Christmas

Coloring Book

Baby
IT'S COLD
Outside

Santa's Workshop
NORTH POLE
HOME
Elf Village
HOLIDAYS
SANTA

Joy

SANTA'S
EXPRESS

Dear Santa,
you are
nice day.
Dear
Santa
Dear Santa,
I wish you could
bring me a dog.

MERRY CHRISTMAS

HO HO HO

SANTA'S
WORKSHOP
24
DEC

Keep warm
and
cozy
this Winter

TOY CHEST
D
$

Made in the USA
Monee, IL
05 December 2022

19809086R00033